How to Set Prices in a Manufacturing Business

A Step by Step Guide to Pricing in a Manufacturing Company

I0462915

By Meir Liraz

Published by BizMove

www.bizmove.com

Table of Contents

1. Introduction

In setting prices in a Manufacturing Firm, the goal should be to maximize profit. Although some owner-managers feel that an increased sales volume is needed for increased profits, volume alone does not mean more profit. The ingredients of profit are costs, selling price, and the unit sales volume. They must be in the proper proportions if the desired profit is to be obtained.

No one set prices formula will produce the greatest profit under all conditions. To price for maximum profit, the owner-manager must understand the different types of costs and how they behave. You need the up-to-date knowledge of market conditions because the "right" selling price for a product under one set of market conditions may be the wrong price at another time.

The "best" price for a product is not necessarily the price that will sell the most units. Nor is it always the price that will bring in the greatest number of sales dollars. Rather the "best" price is one that will maximize the profits of the company.

The "best" selling price should be cost orientated and market orientated. It should be high enough to cover your costs and help you make a profit. It should also be low enough to attract customers and build sales volume.

2. How to Set Optimal Prices

In determining the best selling price, think of price as being like a four layer cake. The four elements in your price are:

(1) the direct costs,

(2) manufacturing overhead,

(3) non-manufacturing overhead, and

(4) profit.

Direct costs are fairly easy to keep in mind. They are the cost of the material and the direct labor required to make a new product. You have these costs for the new product only when you make it.

On the other hand, even if you don't make the new product, you have manufacturing overhead such as janitor service, depreciation of machinery, and building repairs, which must be charged to old products. Similarly, non-manufacturing overhead such as selling and administrative expenses (including your salary) must be charged to your old products.

Direct Costing

The direct costing approach to setting prices enables you to start with known figures when you determine a price for a new product. For example, suppose that you are considering a price for a new product whose direct costs - materials and direct labor - are $3. Suppose further that you set the price at $5. The difference ($5 minus $3 = $2) is "contribution." For each unit sold, $2 will be available to help absorb your manufacturing overhead and your non-manufacturing overhead and to contribute toward profit.

Price-Volume Relationship

Any price above $3 will make some contribution toward your overhead costs which are already there whether or not you bring the product to market. The amount of contribution will depend on the selling price which you select and on the number of units that you sell at that price. Look for a few moments at some figures which illustrate this price-volume-contribution relationship:

Selling Price	$5	$4	$12
Projected sales in units	10,000	30,000	5,000
Projected dollar sales	$50,000	$120,000	$60,000
Direct costs ($3 per unit)	$30,000	$90,000	$45,000
Contribution	$20,000	$30,000	$15,000

In this example, the $4 selling price, assuming that you can sell 30,000 units, would be the "best price" for your product. However, if you could sell only 15,000 units at $4, the best price would be $5. The $5 selling price would bring in a $20,000 contribution against the $15,000 contribution from 15,000 units at $4.

With these facts in mind, you can use a market-orientated approach to set your selling price. Your aim is to determine the combination of selling price and unit volume which will provide the greater contribution toward your manufacturing overhead, non-manufacturing overhead, and profit.

3. Setting Prices Complications

If you ran a non-manufacturing company and could get as much of a product as you could sell, using the direct costing technique to determine your selling price would be fairly easy. Your success would depend on how well you could project unit sales volume at varying selling prices.

However, in a manufacturing company, various factors complicate the setting of a price. Usually, the quantity of a product that you can manufacture in a given time is limited. Also whether you ship directly to customers or manufacture for inventory has a bearing on your production and financial operation. Sometimes your production may be limited by labor. Sometimes by the availability of raw materials. And sometimes by practices of your competition. You have to recognize such factors in order to maximize your profits.

The direct costing concept enables you to key your pricing formula to that particular resource - labor, equipment, or material - which is in the shortest supply. The Gail Manufacturing Company provides an example.

Establish Contribution Percentage

In order to use the direct costing approach, Mr. Gail had to establish a contribution percentage. He set it at 40 percent. From past records, he determined that, over a 12-month period, a 40-percent contribution for each price would take care of manufacturing overhead and profit. In arriving at this figure, Mr. Gail considered sales volume as well as overhead costs.

Determining the contribution percentage is a vital step in using the direct costing approach to pricing. You should review your contribution percentage periodically to be sure that it covers all your overhead (including interest on money you may have borrowed for new machines or for building an inventory of finished products) and to be sure it provides for profit.

Mr. Gails' 40-percent contribution meant that direct costs - material and indirect labor - would be 60 percent of the selling price (100-40=60). Here is an example of how Mr. Gail computed his minimum selling price:

Material   27c
Direct labor   +10c
                   _____
                   37c

The 37 cents was 60 percent of the selling price which worked out to 62 cents (37 cents divided by 60 percent). The contribution was 25 cents (40 percent of selling price):

Selling price   62c
Direct costs   -37c

      ―――――
       25c

In this approach, raw material is given the same importance as direct labor in determining the selling price.

Value of Material

The value of the material used in manufacturing the product has a bearing on the contribution dollars that will accrue from each unit sold. Suppose, in the example above, that the material costs are only 15 cents instead of 27 cents while the direct labor costs remain the same - 10 cents. Total direct costs would be 25 cents.

In order to get a maximum contribution of 40 percent - as Mr. Gail did - the direct costs must not exceed 60 percent of the selling price. To arrive at the selling price, divide the total direct cost by 60 percent (25 cents divided by .60). The selling price is 42 cents. With this new selling price, the contribution is 17 cents (42 cents minus 25 cents for direct costs.)

The point to remember is that when the material costs are less, the contribution will be less. This is true even though the same amount of direct labor and the same amount of machine use is required to convert the raw material into the finished product.

Contribution Per Labor Hour

What happens if Mr. Gail is unable to operate the equipment fully at all time? In order to maximize profits, he must realize the same dollar contribution per direct labor dollar, regardless of the cost materials. To do this, Mr. Gail could use the "Contribution per Labor Hour" Formula for setting his selling prices.

In this formula, you determine a mark-on percentage to use on your direct labor costs. This mark-on will provide the required contribution as percentage of selling price. For example, if direct labor is 10 cents and contribution is 25 cents, then contribution as a percentage of direct labor will be:

$$\frac{25}{10} = 250\%$$

The mark-on factor to use on direct labor costs is 250 percent of direct labor costs.

Now suppose that material is 15 cents and direct labor cost is 10 cents. The selling price would be 50 cents, figured as follows:

Material costs	15c
Direct labor	+10c
	──────
	25c
Contribution	+25c
	──────
Selling Price	= 50c

The "Contribution per Labor Hour" approach assures Mr. Gail a 25 cent contribution for each 10 cents of labor (250 percent) used to make a product regardless of the value of the raw material used.

Contribution-Per-Pound

If, and when, raw materials are in short supply and are the limiting factor, then the base to use is the dollar contribution-per-pound of material. This formula is similar to the one for contribution per labor hour. The difference is that you establish the contribution as a percentage of material cost rather than as a percentage of direct labor cost.

Contribution-Per-Machine-Hour

Determining the contribution-per-machine-hour can be a more involved task than figuring the contribution-per-pound. If different products are made on the same machine, each may use a different amount of machine time. This fact means that the total output of a certain machine in a given time period may vary. As a consequence, the dollar contribution-per-machine-hour that a company realizes may vary from product to product. For example, products A, B, and C are made on the same machine and their contribution-per-machine-hour is:

$28.80 for product A

$26.00 for product B

$20.00 for product C.

When machine capacity is the limiting factor, you can maximize profit by using dollar contribution-per-machine-hour when setting prices. When selling to customers, you should give priority to products that give the greatest dollar contribution-per-machine-hour. In the above example, your sales rep would push product A over products B and C.

To use this pricing approach means that you have to establish a base dollar contribution-per-machine-hour for each machine group. You do it by determining the total number of machine hours available in a given time period. You then relate these machine hours to the manufacturing and non-manufacturing overhead to be absorbed in that period. For example:

Total machine hours available in 12 months = 5,000

Total manufacturing and non-manufacturing overhead = $100,000

Contribution required per machine hour to cover manufacturing

and non-manufacturing overhead = $20*

* $100,000 divided by 5,000 hours

In this example, during periods when the company can sell output of all of its available machine hours, it must realize a return of $20 per machine hour in order to cover its manufacturing and non-manufacturing overhead. When the full 5,000 hours are used, the $20 per-hour return will bring the company to its breakeven point. When all the company's available machine hours cannot be sold, its return per-machine-hour must be more than $20.

Notice that in the above example, only the break even point is considered. There is no provision for profit. How do you build profit into this pricing formula?

Return-on-investments is a good approach. If the Gail Manufacturing Company, for example, has $300,000 invested and wants a 10 percent return, its profit before taxes would have to be $30,000. Mr. Gail can relate this profit goal to the machine-hour approach by dividing the $30,000 by 5,000 (the available machine hours). This means that he needs $6 per machine hour as a mark-up for profit.

Selling Price For Product C

now suppose that Mr. Gail wants to use the contribution-per-machine-hour and profit-per-machine hour approach to set a price for product C. For product C, the direct labor cost per unit is $1.80. Machine output (or units per hour) is 1.25, required contribution per machine hour is $20, and desired profit per machine hour is $6. The formula to set the unit selling price is:

Material cost	21.37
Direct labor	1.80
Contribution per Unit	16.00*
	————
Price before profit	39.17
Desired profit	4.80 ($6 x .80*)
	————
Desired selling price	$43.97

*Calculated as follows: With a machine output of 1.25 units per hour, .80 of a machine hour is needed to produce 1 unit; the required contribution per-machine-hour is $20; therefore, $20 x .80 = $16.

If Mr. Gail is to get a 10 percent return on his investments before taxes, the selling price must be $43.97

But suppose competitive factors mean that Mr. Gail cannot sell product C at $43.97. In such a case, he might:

Not make product C if he can use the machine time to manufacture another product which will give his company its profit of 10 percent - provided, of course, that he has orders for the second product.

Reduce the selling price, if refusing orders for product C means that the machines will be idle. Any price greater than $39.17 will generate some profit which is better than no profit.

But suppose that $39.17 is also too high. Should Mr. Gail turn down all orders for product C at less than $39.17? Not necessarily. If he has no orders to run on the machines, he should accept orders for product C at less than $39.17 because $16 of that price area contributes to manufacturing and non-manufacturing overhead. He has to pay these costs even when the machines are idle.

Keep in mind that the direct costing method of setting a price gives you flexibility. For example, Mr. Gail has to get $43.97 for product C in order to make his desired profit. But his price for that product can range from $23.17 to $43.97 (or higher, depending on market conditions.)

Any price above $39.17 brings in some contribution toward profit. Mr. Gail can break even at 39.17. Any price between $39.17 and $23.17 brings in some contribution toward his overhead. And in a pinch, he can sell as low as $23.17 and recover his direct cost - material and direct labor.

However, Mr. Gail must use this flexibility with care. It takes only a few transactions at $23.17 (recovering only direct costs) to keep him from maximizing profits over a 12-month period.

4. How to Raise Prices Without Losing Customers

Everyone has to increase their prices eventually. If you're fortunate your customers won't notice. But in a budget conscious economy, the chances are they will.

If you run a contract- or consulting-based business, it can be doubly difficult to raise your rates because you're going to have to be upfront about the changes, and in all likelihood negotiate a new contract.

So it all makes for a worrisome situation. However, done right, raising your prices should not alienate your customers – particularly if they value you and your services. Here are some tips for raising your prices without losing customers.

1. Have a Pricing Strategy

A pricing strategy is a well-thought out plan that helps you calculate the prices, rates, or fees associated with your products or services. This may be reviewed monthly, quarterly, or annually depending on market forces, wholesale prices, and other "cost-of-doing-business" expenses. This way you can make rate increases a regular part of your business instead of waiting until it's too late.

2. Change Your Pricing Structure

Changing how you package and price your product or service is a very common way of making more money from customers without a rate hike and without ruffling feathers. Here are some ways to do this:

* Cross-sell Your Services – "Would you like fries with that?" Cross-selling is an easy way to increase sales of related services and meet your customer's needs. For example, a spa business could tag on a range of manicure services to its menu of massage services at a packaged price.

* Tier Your Pricing – Offering multiple price points across your business is a great way to up-sell products and services without raising prices. The plan here is that the tempted consumer will opt for the higher end of the tier. For example, a coffee shop may offer the following options:

1. Cappuccino @ $1.50

2. Cappuccino with a Shot of Syrup @ $2.50

3. Cappuccino with a Shot of Syrup and Cream @ $3.50

The variations are tempting, the value is clearly advertised and the decision to spend more is ultimately in the hands of your customer. The same basic, middle, and premium tiers can also be used in among consulting businesses.

* Change How You Bill Your Time – If you are a consultant or provide any service that involves selling your time in blocks, think about switching how you package your time. Trying to increase your hourly rate can be tough, instead sell your time in different chunks at different rates:

2 hours @ $85 per hour

5 hours @ $75 per hour

10 hours @ $65 per hour

3. What about Consultants or Service-Based Businesses?

If you operate a service-based business or are a freelancer/consultant, consider putting a stake in the ground and raise your rates after you've reached a certain client threshold. Options include raising your rates each year for new customers or after every 5 or 10 new customers, depending on how many clients you have on the books.

In the case of existing customers, approach your client directly and expect to negotiate your rate hike. If you are 100% confident in the value of your services then it's likely that your clients are too and are fully expecting this. Provide a heads up – if you plan on raising your rates in the new year, engage the client in November – this gives them enough time to review your proposed rate, negotiate, and plan accordingly.

4. What if a Customer Balks at the Price Hike?

Everyone has a reason and a right to raise their prices. But be prepared for some push-back and get ready to explain your increase. Explain your price hike in terms of the added value you bring and highlight any investments you have made in yourself (such as training) or your business that justifies the investment.

Above all, expect to negotiate and use your pricing strategy to plan for this. Don't go in too high to start with, because an educated client will almost certainly reject your opening rate without discussion. Likewise, ask yourself how low are you willing to go? What is the ideal mid-point at which you'd be happy to accept a negotiated rate?

5. Calculating Hourly and Project-Based Pricing

If you're a consultant, freelancer or any business that charges by the hour, you are going to have to determine and continuously review your pricing structure. For example, do you charge by the hour? What's a reasonable rate to ask? Are you better off charging clients on a project basis?

Here are some tips for calculating your hourly and project rates and how to negotiate pricing with your client.

1 Determining Your Worth

Deciding what to charge clients is a balancing act between market factors, business costs, and the value you bring to your clients. Before you quote any work, ask yourself these questions:

What is the market rate for work like yours in your industry and location?

How experienced are you? Not just in your line of work, but as a business owner? Being good at a skill is one thing, but being able to manage deadlines, meet expectations and above all, being dependable, are essential qualities for freelancers and consultants.

What rate are you willing to accept and will it cover your costs?

2. Calculating an Hourly Rate

If you've been a salaried employee all your life, making the switch to self-employment requires a change of thinking. Some companies may be tempted to coerce you into a rate that reflects what they'd be willing to pay a salaried employee. But self-employment brings its costs and credit to you. Your rate should reflect this, as well as your expertise.

If you are used to being a salaried employee, here's a good rule of thumb to follow when determining an hourly rate:

Divide your former salary by 52 (work weeks); then divide that number by 40 (the number of work hours in a week). Then mark it up 25-30%.

Your mark-up covers both your value and experience, but also takes care of our business costs such as networking, selling, and other administration, not forgetting your self-employment tax obligations and healthcare insurance costs.

3. Calculating Project Rates

Many clients will prefer to manage their costs and ask for you to price your work as a fixed project fee. This can also work to your benefit, if you price it right. However, it can also work against you, especially if your client is new and the project scope creeps beyond your original expectations.

The best way to calculate project rates is to spend some time scoping out what you'll deliver. For example, if you are a freelance copywriter and a client wants you to price out a two-page white paper, use your knowledge of your own work methods and familiarity with the subject matter to structure your time commitment, for example:

•Research: 2 Hours

•Interview subject matter expert: 1 Hour

•Produce First Draft: 4 Hours

•Two rounds of edits: 2 Hours

Total: 9 Hours @ $x hourly rate = $x

Remember, you don't have to put this calculation in front of your client, but it gives you a useful framework for covering your costs and delivering within scope. Don't forget to add a caveat to address that any work done over and above this scope of work will be charged at an hourly rate

4. Negotiating Your Rate

Negotiation is hard to avoid and can often shed light on whether this is a client that you really want to work with. If you are confident that your pricing reflects your value and the market rate, being haggled hard on price can get a relationship off on the wrong foot. Likewise, being locked in at a low rate can quickly devalue the relationship from your perspective.

So, when it comes to negotiating, be prepared to stand your ground but be willing to compromise. If you foresee further business here, try to be flexible. For example, could you deliver a one-page white paper, instead of two or cut back on the review cycles?

5. What About Retainers?

If a client starts to send a lot of volume your way, retainer-based pricing can be advantageous, even if it's at a lower hourly rate than your advertised price.

A retainer is a fee paid for a pre-determined amount of time or work (usually within a month) and is often paid up-front. A retainer agreement can deliver the benefit of predictable work and income while giving your client the reassurance of having you on "stand-by" and a clear view of monthly costs.

Many consultants charge the full retainer fee, even if they don't work the entire hours allocated. If you value the relationship, steer clear of this; instead, roll unused hours over to next month.